To hunt, hammerheads search by themselves at night. This hammerhead is off to look for its next meal.

Diagram

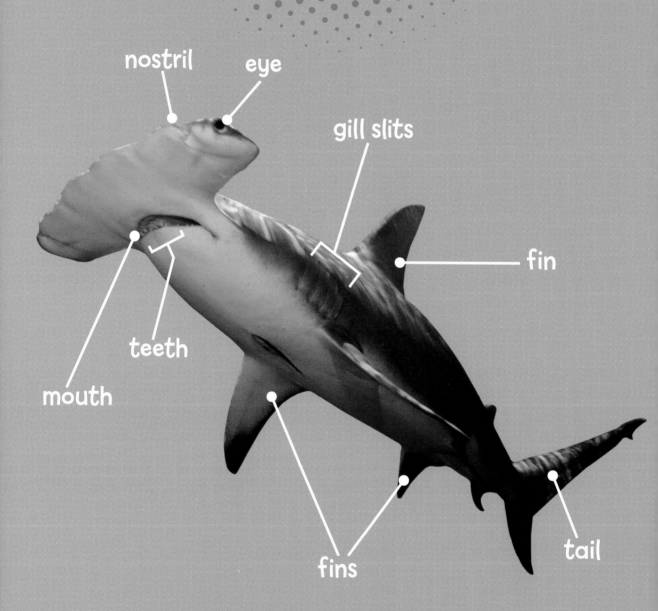

nostril

eye

gill slits

fin

teeth

mouth

fins

tail

Hammerhead Sharks and People

- People are afraid of sharks. But most hammerhead sharks don't attack people. Only three types of hammerhead shark have been known to attack humans.

- People hunt hammerhead sharks for their meat and fins. Some kinds of hammerheads are in danger of dying out.

- Some people are working to save hammerhead sharks. Many countries have rules to protect hammerheads.

Glossary

coast: the land along or near a sea or an ocean

gill: an organ used by fish to get oxygen from water

gill slit: an opening in the sides of a hammerhead shark through which water passes

litter: the young born to an animal at one time

mature: become fully developed

school: a group of fish or other water animals swimming together

Further Reading

Enchanted Learning: Great Hammerhead Shark
http://www.enchantedlearning.com/subjects/sharks/species/Hammerhead.shtml

Franchino, Vicky. *Hammerhead Sharks*. New York: Children's Press, 2015.

Hammerhead Shark Facts for Kids
http://animalstime.com/hammerhead-shark-facts-for-kids-hammerhead-shark-diet-habitat

National Geographic Kids: Hammerhead Shark
http://kids.nationalgeographic.com/animals/hammerhead-shark

Silverman, Buffy. *Great White Sharks in Action*. Minneapolis: Lerner Publications, 2018.

Wilsdon, Christina. *The Wonderful World of Sharks*. New York: Disney, 2012.

Index

Photo Acknowledgments

The images in this book are used with the permission of: © Martin Strmiska/Alamy, pp. 2, 5, 6, 7; © Ken Kiefer/Getty Images, p. 4; © ArteSub/Alamy, p. 8; © David Fleetham/naturepl. com, p. 9; © Andre Seale/Alamy, p. 10; © Martin Strimska/Moment Open/Getty Images, p. 11; © Gerard Soury/Minden Pictures, p. 12; © Mark Conlin/Alamy, pp. 13, 20; © imageBROKER/ Alamy, p. 14; © Alex Mustard/Minden Pictures, p. 15, 19; © Cultura Creative/Alamy, p. 16; © Rich Carey/Shutterstock.com, p. 17; © WaterFrame/Alamy, p. 18; © Alex Mustard/Getty Images, p. 19; © Wildestanimal/Alamy, p. 22.

Front cover: © Martin Strmiska/Alamy.

Main body text set in Billy Infant regular 28/36. Typeface provided by SparkType.

Hammerhead Sharks in Action

Benjamin Tunby

Lerner Publications • Minneapolis

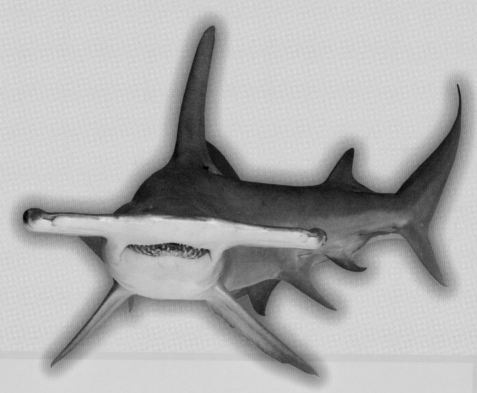

Lerner Publications Company
A division of Lerner Publishing Group, Inc.
241 First Avenue North
Minneapolis, MN 55401 USA

For reading levels and more information, look up this title at www.lernerbooks.com.

Library of Congress Cataloging-in-Publication Data

Names: Tunby, Benjamin, author.
Title: Hammerhead sharks in action / Benjamin Tunby.
Description: Minneapolis : Lerner Publications, [2017] | Series: Lightning bolt books. Shark world | Audience: Ages 6-9. | Audience: K to grade 3. | Includes bibliographical references and index.
Identifiers: LCCN 2016039577 (print) | LCCN 2016045519 (ebook) | ISBN 9781512433791 (lb : alk. paper) | ISBN 9781512455953 (pb : alk. paper) | ISBN 9781512450620 (eb pdf)
Subjects: LCSH: Hammerhead sharks—Juvenile literature. | CYAC: Sharks.
Classification: LCC QL638.95.S7 T86 2017 (print) | LCC QL638.95.S7 (ebook) | DDC 597.3/4—dc23

LC record available at https://lccn.loc.gov/2016039577

Manufactured in the United States of America
1-42015-23885-11/9/2016

Table of Contents

A Big Fish

A great hammerhead shark looks for food near the ocean floor. It has a flat, T-shaped head. It spends most of its time hunting.

Great hammerhead sharks are the largest kind of hammerhead. There are eight other kinds too.

Hammerhead sharks have five pairs of gill slits.

Hammerhead sharks are a kind of fish. Fish open their mouths to take in water. Gills take oxygen from the water. Then the water goes out of the fish through gill slits.

Hammerhead sharks live in oceans all around the world. Many live in warm water near the coasts of Costa Rica, Hawaii, eastern Africa, and southern Africa.

Hammerhead sharks often stay in places with lots of food.

Scientists aren't sure how many hammerhead sharks there are. The sharks live deep underwater, so it is tough to count them.

Baby Sharks

Baby hammerhead sharks grow in eggs inside their mother's body. After about eleven months, the eggs hatch. The mother gives birth to a litter of live baby hammerhead sharks.

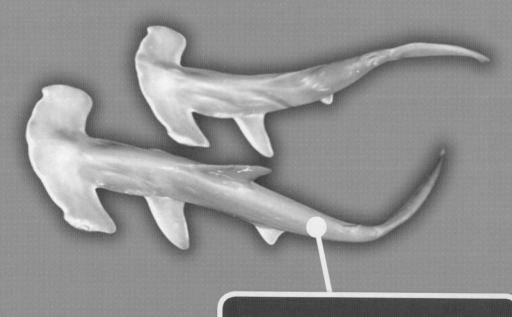

Baby hammerhead sharks are called pups.

A litter is usually between six and forty-two pups. At birth, pups can be 27 inches (69 centimeters) long. That's about as long as a tennis racket.

The mother shark does not stay with her pups. They can already swim and find their own food. The pups will stay together until they are strong enough to head to deeper waters.

Hammerhead sharks can live for twenty to thirty years.

The sharks can have babies of their own once they mature. Great hammerhead sharks are usually mature when they reach 7.5 to 10 feet (2.3 to 3 meters) in length.

Wide-Angle View

Adult hammerheads can be as long as 20 feet (6 m). Their powerful tails help them move through the water.

Hammerhead sharks are known to make quick turns. They have many fins to help them control their movements.

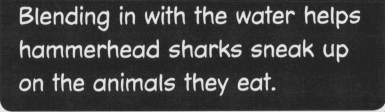

Blending in with the water helps hammerhead sharks sneak up on the animals they eat.

Hammerhead sharks have a white belly and a dark back. The white belly helps hide them when viewed from below. Their dark back helps them blend in with the dark ocean floor.

A hammerhead shark's eyes are on the sides of its wide head. This allows the sharks a wide-angle view to look for food.

Hammerhead sharks also have powerful senses of hearing and smell to help them find food.

Hammerhead sharks have a small mouth for their size. Their teeth are sharp and jagged. They need them to bite their food into smaller chunks. *CHOMP!*

Hunting Alone

A lot of animals live deep in the ocean where hammerhead sharks swim. A hammerhead shark eats shrimp, squid, and small fish.

Hammerheads may eat other sharks, including smaller hammerheads.

Hammerhead sharks often eat stingrays. The sharks use the front of their head to pin a stingray against the ocean floor. Then the stingray cannot use its stinger.

Hammerheads will sometimes travel in schools of up to five hundred sharks.

During the day, hammerhead sharks move in groups called schools. The school helps protect the hammerheads from larger sharks.